A Most Improbable Life

Poems by
Gabriella Gutiérrez y Muhs

Finishing Line Press
Cincinnati • Georgetown

Copyright © 2002 by Gabriella Gutiérrez y Muhs
ISBN 0-9726136-6-8
First Edition

All rights reserved under International and Pan-American Copyright Conventions. No part of this book may be reproduced in any manner whatsoever without permission from the publisher, except in the case of brief quotations embodied in critical articles and reviews.

Acknowledgements

California -- published in Cruzando Puentes: Antología de Lit. Latina, UCSB in Spanish, 2001
Rosary Beads – Published in The Latin American Studies Journal, Stanford Univ. 2000.
Pillow Talk – Published in The 25th Anniversary Anthology, Bilingual Review, 1998.
De Corazón- Published in The 25th Anniversary Anthology, Bilingual Review, 1998.
California Too – Published in Quarry West: Poets and Writers of the Monterey Bay Anthology, Ed. Ken Weisner, 2000.
12th Commandment by a Mexican Woman-- Published in The 25th Anniversary Anthology, Bilingual Review, 1998.

Editor: Leah Maines
Cover Design and Inside Photos: Eric Muhs
Cover Art: María Luisa Romero and Eric Muhs

Printed in the USA.
e-mail: finishingl@aol.com
Author inquires and orders:
        Finishing Line Press
        P.O. Box 1626
        Georgetown, Kentucky 40324

Dedicatoria

In the mural of my eyelids you remain imprinted, bold musas luchadoras de oro whose ideals I shall never forget, whose words and actions have cracked open the world
Cecilia Preciado Burciaga, Carmen González, Connie Anthony, Kari Lerum, Shirley Flores-Muñoz, Yvonne Yarbro-Bejarano.
En agradecimiento, amor y lealtad para mi mamá Socorro Favela Rivera, y con cariño para mis tíos Ramón y Luz Favela Rivera, los cuates.With an open heart singing for the joy of knowing you, to my other mother Debbie Carver Muhs.
Con el corazón de solidaridad y amor para mi hermana Yolanda Gutiérrez Miller. Para/Por mis tres amores eternos, they who never leave the screen of life:
Eric, Eleuterio, Enrico Muhs.
A las musas esenciales: Jeanette Rodríguez, Yolanda G. Miller, Patrice Vecchione, María Luisa Romero, Elyane Gentili, Lupita Vega, Shirley Flores Muñoz, Melyssa Jo Kelly, Adriana C. Berchenko, Sandra Ramírez (Cindy),Coco Pellerino, Sheilah Serfaty, Lisa Wescott, Lila Martín, Demetria Martínez, Roberta Armenta, Olga Díaz, Norma Cantú
A las siempre comadres y madrinas: Jeanette Rodríguez, Lucía Ochoa Nuñez, Yolanda Gutiérrez Miller, Olga López Valero Colbert, Laura Piñón, Graciela Vega, Rhonda Peters, Yvonne Yarbro-Bejarano, Victoria Lugo, Shirley Flores-Muñoz, A los grandes amigos: Alex Flores, David Thorn, Ray Pellerino, Valentín Ferdinán, Dan Goldberg, Ted Fortier, Antonio López Valero, Randy Colbert, Mark Parsons, Ramón Silva, especialmente Jesús Rosales.

Para todos mis familiares, y muy especialmente para mis sobrinas Emilia, Allegra y Mónica. For aunts and uncles: Biv and Ed Walker, Kas Kuhn, y mis tías Delfina, Carmen, Rosario, Refugio, Manuela y todos los primos primeros y segundos. A los buenos amigos: Humberto Valdivia Sandoval, Sonny Acosta, Francisco Velásquez, Noé Gonzalez, Paul Caryotakis, Alfonso Anaya, Marc McLeod, Perry Phillips, Bob Olona, Jean Umbert Gentili, Robert Hinrix, Ben Olguín, Robert Nuñez, Jeff Greinke, Michael Torrey y Miguel López Rojo. A las buenas amigas: Myrna Stone, Vera Romandía, Missie Olona, Kerri Sinclair, Imme Bergmeier, Eleanor Kuser, Susan Hendrickson, Isabelle Liberto, Jane Marie Yett, Sharon Suh, Peggy Morrison, Eileen Driscoll, Dawn DeGroot, Roshi Sirjani-Shamloo, Jacalyn Harden, Lydia Camarillo, Carla Faini, Minette Riordan, Alicia Camacho Schmidt, Maria Cotera, Susana Gallardo, Tisa Carrillo, Nani Carillo, Leticia Bermudez, Maud Nadiré, Antonia García. To my high school lifelines: Penny Pannabaker, Nancy Tanimasa, Kathy Asai, Allan Tao, Fred Holybee, Lety and Ramiro Rodríguez, Kathy Lynch, Susan Russo, Cathy Faduska, Beth Margo. los/las abrecaminos,: José Antonio Burciaga, Karen Mary Dávalos, Chon Noriega, Sandra Cisneros, Cherrie Moraga, Adrianne Rich, Lorna Dee Cervantes, Marjorie Agosín, Francisco X. Alarcón, Jeff Tagami, Shirley Ancheta, Frank Bardache, Julie Olsen Edwards, Tillie Olsen, Ada Sosa Ridell, Dennis Morton, Antonia Castañeda, Ekua Omosupe, Sherman Alexie, Denise Chávez. A los profesores: Don Luis Leal, David Bugé, Ken Atchity, Lauro Flores, Mary Louise Pratt, Traise Yamamoto, John Laue, Annabelle Rea, Claire Fox, Michael Predmore, Jack Raper, Len Davies, Manuel Macías, Karen Vanderdool, Art Pearl, Paz Haro, Camillo Penna. A los que sin conocerme creyeron en mí; Maria Teresa Woytheller, Karen Warren, Lalena Vann, Marina Cook, Ane Marie Parks, Lety Camacho, George Ow, Gail Knaap. A mis muertos: José de Jesús Gutiérrez, Gelacio Favela, Marco Favela, Francisco Lopes, Mike Sullivan, Elsie Wilcox, John Muhs, Guadalupe Favela, Francisca Favela Rivera, Ana María Sosa Delgado, Francisco y Eleuterio Favela. A todos mis estudiantes muy especialmente a Ayva Larson que caminó conmigo el sendero de las letras y a Beth Oretsky. A las familias de Jean Claude y ElyaneGentili y Pablo y Adriana Berchenko en Francia, Juan José y Magdalena Sosa Delgado en Durango México, Horst Zerweck en Monthey Suiza, Mariano y Angelines López Valero en Madrid, Serapia y Asunción Vega en Watsonville, California, Pedro Y Mercedes Martín en San José, Ca., Familia de Adilia Rojas en San José, Costa Rica y especialmente para mi editora Leah Maines. My healers: Winfield Hobbs, Mark Jyringi, Eileen Driscoll.

Contents

Unconditionality 7
White flags don't cry peace all the time 8
Hotel Isabel (In Room 313) 9
The Anthropologist 10
Empty Moon or My Mother's Molcajete is a Black Hole . 12
Nada(ando) 13
Shopping 14
I Miss the Cold 15
There's a run in my heart 16
Cyberman 18
Amor Filial en los 90s 19
A Most Improbable Life 20
Antarctica 22
Los Hombres de Tierra 23
Diaspora 24
De Corazón 25
She's Come Out of Bakery Calendars 26
December 27
Fractions 29
Libros 30
En un día lluvioso 31
My Country 33
Medusa 34
El Otro Lado 35
Pillow Talk 36
Seatl-Nahuatl (to Seattle, the land of lakes, Aztlán) ... 37
Rosary Beads 39
A Measure of your heart is with St. Francis amiga, but you are not St. Claire 40
Sobre 41
My son thinks we are cows 42
Don't Misunderstand Her! 43
They are mixed, they are charros in a car! 44
Angela Davis and I 46
Invaluable Tears or Professional Woman 47
My Brown Toyota and Me Over 17 48
Guadsunvil 49

Curandera/Community Nurse	50
My Freedoms	51
I Never Had A Picture Of My Parents/Surtout	52
The 12th Commandment by a Mexican Woman	53
Their Country	54
California: Fresh as a Lettuce	55
California Too	56
Sor Juana's Children	57
When I was a Wetback	58
Enchiladas, Entomatadas, Chilaquiles	60
Oda a Jose Antonio Burciaga en Tres Partes	61
About the Author	62
Finishing Line Press	63

Unconditionality

It is the unconditionality
of culture
that pervades me,
the sweetness of the smile
of destiny
upon my witnessed hand

that uncanny exactness
that directs the tattoo
from my wounded eye,
the stroll of lights unconscious
towards the ancient steps
that titillates the sorrow
from my fermented soul

the weakness of the highway
that disconnects my path

the stroll of memories
that refurbishes
dreams in cages,

the irrefutable precision
of confusion
that strengthens the direction
of my kite

White flags don't cry peace all the time

My heart is a floating piece of ice
in someone's mind.
I am no longer human in the rain.
I disappear in the breath of re-creation,
Politically correct
Middle class tongues sculpt me in their image
I recognize only myself
in the pupils of your kindness.

The fillings in your teeth
are precious stones
that absorb the shock
of glaciers
Unloved
by their mothers.

Could white be white
in the desert?
or does it disappear into
auroras cracked by our jeep?
Does the sun ever play insomnia
in your heart?
or do you make it wear a white flag
in its right pocket?
Do handkerchiefs go blind?

Hotel Isabel (In Room 313)

During the day for ten pesos your name inscribed on a
grain of rice,
For two dollars, solidarity with the hotel bus man,
uninterrupted diurnal counseling services from the
receptionist,
calm.

by unknown betrayal,
my heart pounding like a choo choo,
my mental paper filled with exes,
my left knee feeling sorry for itself.

all notions of lost grief,
all endings of a first book
unread by vision,
drumming breath sleeping on the bed.

All, a traveler's nightmares in a dream,
all, itches for a fingerless scratch.

In the lobby of my dawn,
sleepless fish on anti depressants,
common accidents of urban life,
the adjacent disco pounding with my heart
to the beat of a fragmented city's hand shake,

A kite flying in the dark.

a phone call ringing to the disco beat,
to the flying incarcerated fish,
my son sleeping on the bed,

a sleepless kite anxious for a smogless breath.

The Anthropologist

All he wanted was skeleton
to count the bones;
one bone for every day he loved,
left without uttering a word.

Should we really be shaped
in the image of
curves?
like Chevy's in the 50's,
immune to squares
or lines
symptomatically spiral
glowing in the dark
for love to stretch
the truth from us.

All he wanted were the smiles
of non-fleshed us
in skulls with perfect teeth
before they could hurt,
with muscles
eliciting words.

He wanted bones he could heal
from the solitude of dirt,
bones he could line up
like notes before the composer,
notes that could be
heard by looking,
notes that didn't end at the beginning,
Love notes to give his lover.

Mexicans would say

"He loved her bones,"
but the anthropologist
couldn't
because
really what he loved
was the image her bones
imprinted on his spirit
the image of love
before it's disinterred.

Empty Moon or My Mother's Molcajete is a Black Hole

The moon is her mole,
only comes out
when it's dark in her soul.

She only fills the moon
with broken bread, migas
when it is empty.

Only cooks for her books;
unkept children,
pans without titles.

Only eats the moon
on Sundays during mass.
Only sails her yacht
on the clouds through rosaries,
only reads when she remembers,
only sees when she forgets
forgives while sweeping
polka dots into shape
the size of moles
on the moon,
molcajete craters.

Nada(ando)
Three possible translations: Swimming, I have nothing, I wear nothing
For Shirley Flores-Muñoz

The woman strokes her self
in the water,
stroke by stroke
her swimming erases the unrepairable words on the
board.

She stretches back into the womb
of the mother
inside her,
there is no counselor like water
she thinks
as she theorizes
a recovery of her self
knowing
that after spending nine months inside her
no child could be born wrong.

She caresses the water
in her
floating novels and poems she read.
Soon books are cellophane floating around her
cushioning her
from the so very concrete world.
She thinks:
"If water could only have hands
instead of this
beautiful rhythm as body,
I wouldn't need a man".

Shopping

She lookin' for a dress that doesn't fit
so she can bring it back.

She lookin' for a moment by herself
many years ago
when something she happened to.

She lookin' for a talk show host
she'll never see again
so her three pounds of current grief
will fall on her counter- disappear

She lookin' for body parts she wants to buy
so she can bring them back,
exchange them for parts untouched by any relatives or
friends or significant
others- untouched by flesh or vegetables.

She lookin' for underwear clean,
without sperm or blood, or male pubic hairs or someone
else's oppression, or
stains or thoughts or books or novels or old cartoons.

She lookin' for a ring
that fits the vacuum cleaner,
to request her hand in marriage.

She lookin' for Styrofoam
clean as the clouds in Mary Had a Little Lamb
soft as the toughness of cotton.

She lookin' for a soul
clean as a shiny mall.

I Miss the Cold

When they had the cold war
we were hot chocolate and tamales.
Luke warm behavior lined up in degrees for recent
immigrants and others,
their coldness towards the cold unknown,
the cold of tundras
and black markets
the cold of vegetables frozen
and iron cold.

The cold was a war of weather for those who didn't
know where was the cold.
It meant that war was measurable
and beginning and ending and that there was a middle
templado.

I miss the cold war
in measurements, degrees and barometers
the justefiedly outside,
the walls of heartless barrios warm
known and interior.

This warmth of
papers, politics, pan o palo (bread or stick)
peppers my eyes
into a shiny terror.

There's a run in my heart

They have taken a nail
and scratched out the meaning of me
with the label of ingredients

My heart has a run
that I can't stop
hiding under inequality and class,
chipped tongues that flap

Nail polish does not work,
the needle is too big for the thread,
the color too thick to swallow
They buffet
On the red jello
oozing out of the
Run----I collect it
For writing
Red was never imaginary ink

I caulk the wounds with sadness,
It always works
A rendition of Jane Sibery accompanies the wound
"prepare the run for repair" mother yells
she sauters culture onto its crevices
sculpts sayings from shattered rivets
and states "the physical work is finished
now you must weave the run unto itself--- reinforce the
material without showing any stitches--- The Mexican
way,

Hoping there are
Others
who know how to reweave
a running heart into perfection
I take the seeping heart
and start weaving embroidery,
camouflage
before
Hearts' running thread
I meditate two breaths at a time,
I cease
¿Will the run ever stop?
¿Will the hose of my reflection
run onto itself?
¿Will I be disintegrated into
the saliva of cheap tongues?
¿Will the soldering, caulking, sculpting
Of love
stop the run?

Cyberman

Did I lose a poem in your screen?

Did the sun ever set on the dolphin climber's hand?

Will there be porridge
for the three pigs
who sit on the board of trustees to your illegal dreams?

to your documented love,
to your web site on a cloud
to your green house in the Internet
to your tortured avenue of love

Does the labyrinth in your heart need a magnet to explore itself?

Have the flowers on your keypad run away from your fingers?

will there be peace on the hard disk after the search is deleted?

will a woman/man ever enter through the chair sitting next to you, or will s(he) have to make him/herself a Window wo(man), a married widow, a Cinderella looking for the slipper in your Word documents?

are your friends too late to find you?

Amor Filial en los 90s
  Para Olga Colbert

Los últimos recuerdos que tengo de tí
no son los últimos, ni los primeros los últimos
Son recuerdos de objetos, caras, pensamientos
música, poemas por dentro, por fuera de tí,
la cara iluminada, los zapatos viejos, las roommates.

Son recuerdos de cariño amplificado, corazones plenos,
amores de novela, tú, la televisión.
Son recuerdos de computadoras que lloran a nuestros pies
rogándonos que hagamos el amor con ellas, otro trabajo,
tocándoles las teclas de redención.

Son niños paridos, llorando de gusto por salir de tí,
padres viajantes, como cartas, por avión.

Son lechos, papeles, almas caminantes, museos, entierros,
llaves y carpas, piedras, mares y cubiertas
de amistades y amor.
Son piedras maltratadas, ecos irrumpidos
Seattle en una manga, Paris en la otra,
y en medio tus pechos dando de mamar.

Los últimos recuerdos que tengo de tí, no son los primeros
ni los primeros los últimos. Los últimos no existen y los primeros
crecen como pinos de Navidad.

Son velas que se apagan,
Son el infinito,
Son el amor!

"It seems to me that I have lived a most improbable life, one which by turns blesses and bewilders me." (181) "The Province of Radical Solitude", Carolyn Forché

A Most Improbable Life

I missed The Yale Series of Younger Poets Award,
the Fulbright Dissertation Fellowship,
I will never be a Rhodes Scholar,
my poetry was not international
like Carolyn Forché's.
I only write about my father
whom nobody else loved
a fallen leaf in Spring
a no one missed him kind of guy,
the dirty laundry water that washed and fed
the mouths of three generations
of apple eaters
over and under a tree,
a Noone.

My father did not write
poems
he did not know
what poems were
except at 5 when I was six
coming out of my mouth
Amado Nervo's
"Me gusta la lima,
me gusta el limón
pero más me gusta
salir de excursión."
He chuckled while I recited this,
because he did not understand
"excursión" and the word tickled him
only coming out of my mind.

A Noone
he died like Edgar Allan Poe
drunk under a table in a bar.
But he was not a poet,
and in a caste system
I would not be a poet.

I would only clean beans
and feed oats to the animals
on a good planting year.
I could only write books that were mountains
read stomachs that were hunger,
theorize about the cycles of life,
knit baby shoes for new life,
live a "common" life.

Today I live as far removed from my childhood
as Hollywood has always been.
I live a life of paper
not chiles rellenos
or dried husk pens,
a life of ink
that longs for octopus fairy tales
a life of plastic
in bed and kitchens
screens and cars.
I hold plastic animals
fed with paper
tamed with ink
all small replacements of love?
all parts of an unorthodox
unfolding
an improbable life.

Antarctica

Gestation takes eighteen months for a continent,
we birthed Antarctica in your heart
She now walks on people's computers
eats time, cell minutes are dedicated to her
She is a fine young woman
in two years.
Her wisdom has aged
me-- Atlas will no longer help me
with the world,
come back!
The boys watching TV, cartooning
Are you in your TV watching the boys watching cartoons?
Today is not the beginning of their solitude
They understand your voyage
They know of dark wet places they needed to reside in
in order to be lit
for this they love the dryness, brightness of cartoons
They watch Sponge Bob
under water living like you,
they watch cartoons
an image digitized in your brain
only
they have grown
awaiting white postcards
from the bottom of the world.
Antarctica, the A hanging from their foreheads because
they have adulterated
your image—you are still larger than a house
But, they could not wait
to grow
multiplication tables, division, teeth, semblances of
civilization in their backpacks
book crumbs through Spiderman's thumbs, liking
Katherine, a hundred movies
older they are, than last month.

Los Hombres de Tierra
 En Agradecimiento, inspirado por Octavio Villalpando

Men of earth
are mushrooms.
They cure winds that pass over them
and softly touch what oddly touches them.
They only speak in words
that ring like bells,
like bells few words,
that carry sound
beyond their quick horizons
Men of earth
clean worlds with their presence
and go on
to titillate the world
with their hearts
Men of earth
remunerate others with their souls
like spring water
they mantra
spirits with their silence
and sterilize
auras with their absence
Men of earth among us
give kisses to the universe
in written words,
shake hands
with East and West
as forgotten Ghandis
in our closets,
traverse dishonesty
and open doors
to other men of earth.

Diaspora

Are tears the salt that stops us from drying up?,
or are they the love we cannot express?
Are they a plus or a minus, an addition or a subtraction?
a poem or a curse?

Are our tears the myths we chose to believe in?
or the ironies we could never touch?

Do our tears take us back to the womb?
or do we deliver them
as food to our changes?

Are they liquid thoughts we never will get to write,
or oceans we will never visit?

De Corazón

    I
And she,
my mother
need not write books,
for her ink
has fallen on industrial pages,
it is no chisel
but blood can mark.

    II
Her word is with her once a month,
as she walks her work on her back,
her word has the power to turn into education,
her care into people of loyalty.

    III
I'll continue to write from the blood she lends me,
joyfully,
from the hand of what might have been another sibling.

She's Come Out of Bakery Calendars

1950: My mother's picture at the Villa dressed of China Poblana
on her right standing, a painting of the Virgin of Guadalupe,
on her left, her sister Guadalupe sitting,
watching her sister be a standing China Poblana
at the Villa, next to a picture of the tilma guadalupana
The Mexican Mecca
One could not pile on wishes without the other.
1968: The Virgin has a coming out party. She comes out of the church,
through Tlatelolco, women standing in red October with pictures of
their killed sons and husbands, disappeared by the Olympics,
only the picture of the Virgin is out, only she dries impotent, ink tears.
1990: She's come out of bakery calendars. She's wearing herself in high hills,
on cars, walls, and people tatoos: kung fu fighting,
jogging, sewing. She's a modern woman, soon a waitress to be
from a country where sirens are books
She rides on steering wheels and mirrors, rubs a pregnant women's stomach,
hugs a drunk, sits next to homeless people on the bus, visits museums with them
to see herself on Amalia Mesa Bains, Yolanda and Alma López, or on Esther Hernández' stage,
still walks the dead to the four year underground limbo, the Mictlán with small business cards.
2000: She settles for people wearing black
artists, widows, introspective sort of people,
people who wouldn't buy pan dulce
in January and get a panadería calendar,
people who know how to smell fresh baked bread
but cannot open the door to a bakery,
She CEO's large institutions of people who pray to her by e-mailing wishes to other sad people in offices.

December

December was a happy month for most Mexicans, but not in our house, no posadas, no aquinaldos, tejocotes only at church,
we only prayed, the Virgin somber, her apparition brought no joy,
only sad presents without Rudolph, snow men or Santo Clos

Our hearts were not Piñatas waiting to be broken, they were somber.
Our house was where my mom's house went
because she was the non alcoholic, she was the house
because she was the one at home who fed us and nurtured us most of the time,
she was the one to tell lies to
to not tell lies to.

Thirty years later in my house where My Virgin of Guadalupe smiles, eats
buñuelos, and tells jokes in December,
I find out the sadness of death my father carried in his right hand
having killed a man on the 12th
with the same hand he caressed apples,
the same hand he drunk his liver with
the same hand he believed by drinking his celebration of the Virgin's miracles to
disappear
the same hand that smelled roses away from our house,
they reminded him years past of a celebration when a man who tried to kill him had died.

She told by not telling , she didn't want to remember.

Thirty years later my mother murmurs under breath
that Xmas only brings her sadness, stupor, sniffles
my grandfather died on Xmas day
and she has never cried enough for him.
I lead her into a crying mantra
on Xmas day.
The Birth of Jesus, the death of the Father,
so much pain for both,
Xmas lights are roads to lead them to heaven.

All the wonderings of truth and how December would
have been different:
Santo Clos not buried in shame and pain, but floating in
salty tears
forgiveness, a crying candle
mourners' pains coming down the rain on Xmas,
like snow in the East coast over shingle roofs, brick
colored, dirt colored
scars in a calendar.

Fractions

A third of
one life
is almost
half of another

The best of my
life is almost
all the hope,
mystery, tears,
laughter and happiness
with you.

A third of
your life
is almost
all of mine.

Libros
    dedicado a los que se han comido su biblioteca

La tortilla como libro,
Libro de mano izquierda
como una Frida en cinta,
o una limosnera rica.
como quien no sabe
que los libros son
margenes escritos por los pobres.
Libro canto, canto libro,
hecho de tortillas de harina,
con tinta de niño bolero,
resbaloso,
zapatero,
imprenta de visiones,
pesadillas,
zapatos por bolear, en
cualquier esquina de un recuerdo,
las tortillas de harina.
Libro del saber que
hubiera podido escribir,
imprimir,
redimir,
el pulquero de México que
aquí es esquirol.
Libro sin dientes,
con sonrisas,
con corrientes de papel,
lisas
por los años de ser
comparado con el pan
BIMBO.

No te tenemos.
No te podemos meter en
lo más profundo
de la ciencia,
de la ciencia de la señora
que vende todavía,
pantalones de casa en casa.
De la ciencia de los que
no alcanzan, de los que no pueden,
de los que no saben,
lavarse los dientes.
Libro de media tarde
cuando la gente sale de trabajar.
Libro de medianoche
cuando al no poder dormir
jugamos a las canicas con
la mente.
Y porqué no?
Libro decente,
de los que dicen, de los
que saber que
"debemos hablar mejor."
Libro de la gente.
Libro de las manzanas.
Libro para cualquier
ocasión o cualquier día.
 Libro como baile de un
huérfano al que se le
olvidó la cumbia.
Libro de mano izquierda,
cobija de los pobres.

En un día lluvioso

Estoy tan triste
que podría con una de mis lágrimas
hundir la pluma que te escribe.

El velo de tristeza de disfraza.
Porque la ilusión es el escaparate
de todas la mentiras.

La tristeza es la indolencia
que nos acaricia con menos
autenticidad y más ternura.
El tubo de escape.

"Lindsey Wagner, you are not the real bionic woman, my friend Lupe is"

For Lupita Vega

My TV the temple,
Lindsay Wagner, the saint
Tuesday night fight
in the ring with dad
Bionic Woman or Animals in the Wild

At times I won,
Lindsay Wagner
the heroine impostor, gliding over cars
she had no plastic knees
titanium elbows,
shoulders, hips, like you do.

Lindsay Wagner
no scars to show on her pages white as an empty journal
no morphene dreams
or ribbons, as your mother calls your scars
no wisdom about pain,
No, I'd rather read you.

Lindsay does not grow people with her words
or chase pain away with one look
or pray for Deepak Chopra, and his pain.

The parenthesis on your knees
like all the books you've read, scars
trees lined up, roads yielding feelings out of your body.

The skin on your hips fits over you like a tupperware cup
sealing you
so you can walk,
so you can find more ribbons in your path.

My Country

My son
the country I wished for,
the institution
where milk flows through
from north to south
Organization
of all tongues,
no longer two parties
a flag of all flags
a continent of trees extinct
a river of red
that is not blood
of courage that is not war
of freedom that is not money,
a self contained ocean that is my son,
a country run by love.

Medusa

Her hair was curly,
question marks unlimited.
Not only her pubic hairs
but all her shields.
Her mustache grew fine
over her eyes
breath and sight together,
speaking a long line of armors
razors, wax and tweezers.

Why do we always
mutilate our growth?
she asked
in unison with her
other voice,
the hairless voice
that was cold and needy.

Hairs, she thought, are
the body's punctuation,
as she spread Neet
over her thoughts.

El Otro Lado
At my grandmother's house when someone died they went to "El Otro Lado." If they went to work while we were in México, they went to El Otro Lado. If my uncles went to visit relatives, their wives in the winter while in the U.S., they went to "El Otro Lado."

I never understood where El Otro Lado was.
I learned to read maps at an early age,
to find out EL OTRO LADO

A mouth, a bean, a heart, all look alike from afar
In el otro lado, taste different
settle in you like an incrusted ring
into your finger
a mouth kissing, purring words out like a dove
a bean not of Jack in the bean stalk
a heart, an ace, a lone arranger
Like a deck of cards or the folds of an accordion El Otro Lado hid,
behind a river over a mountain
under a dream that was American
and Mexican and holy
El otro lado
a bigger unanswered prayer that we find
only in conversation, a U.A. a Mexico, a universe, an underground, the skies and the heavens all in one continent
like the holy US spirit
father Mexico
son death
a triptych trinity of thoughts
Aztlán
I learned to read maps at an early age
only to understand death has countries and rivers and mountains
death has flowers and lava volcanoes
death has mothers and fathers and trees of all matters
Del Otro Lado

Pillow Talk

When I was growing up a pillow was a human being's most noted possession.
They always wore a nice dress, pillows that is.
My mother embroidered and taught us to embroider silk flowers on their face, like people they wear masks.
My sister's pillow case matched mine, my moms' matched my father's, that's how we knew they were married, and we,
my sister and I, have been married ever since.
In my family we carried everything we owned in one pillow.
If it fit inside the pillow it was yours; if it didn't it was someone else's.
Pillows have many compartments and many smells.
By inspecting their corners you know their personalities:
Jean stuffed braveheart pillows,
soft, tender, feminine side pillows,
coffee dregs, grouchy pillows,
cushion memory pillows,
stomach aching pepto bismol pillows,
accident prone, sybil pillows,
puppet draining pillows,
tooth decay, hospital linen pillows,
among many.
My mother never washed the side of her pillow my grandmother laid on every year, before we left her for nine months.
What we remember about my grandma is still the memory of a ten month odor. My mother's house is a pillow factory or better yet, a pillow designer's nightmare.
Pillows born there don't have names or ideas or even corners.
They have a strong conviction and a distinct identity, they know they'll end up meeting an owner.
I asked my mother why she made so many pillows and had none. She said to me: "I'm privileged, but if I weren't, the only thing I'd like to own is a pillow. My pillows are like a computer that saves dreams for others to sleep with.

Seatl-Nahuatl (to Seattle, the land of lakes, Aztlán)
For Lauro Flores

Fall

October in Seattle,
the leaves
of space needles
wrestle with the rain
through the window-shopping eyes
of spirits,
visions threaded
from above,
Desde el Más Allá

Winter

Winter snow
shelters
traffic lights
to shine like Xmas trees
on homeless quilts.

Spring

The city
simmers
herbal flower teas
on its streets
of always water.

Summer

Parking garages
sizzle
like refrying bean oil
cars
the cheese-like profiles
of Scandinavians,
happy to park
across the street
from the sun.

Rosary Beads

Laid out like rosary beads
in malls
the men minding monsters
afraid of them
holding on to the scapulary
that lassoes them in
to clean yards,
build self-esteem,
build a middle class.

They lay
like rosary beads
tied by a thread
of need
and hope
and trust
and hunger
and strength,
the five mysteries

of a rosary.

A Measure of your heart is with St. Francis amiga, but you are not St. Claire

A measure of your heart is
Slowly singing
Slowly spying on your brain.

You are not the duchess
of his hollow teeth,
His breath belongs
to a Virgin statue
on the corner of life.

And you can't imagine
when the tea kettle
rung like an alarm clock
to find you sprayed by love
in a cookie jar.

Your heart is braided
like a crop,
unto the veins of destiny.
You are an elephants' trunk
about to use all its muscles
except you

You are not the measure
of a heart
poured in a gallon.
Your heart
belongs tattooed, transplanted,
grafted, digitized,
unto his picture,
unto his life.

Sobre
Para Carmen Gonzalez y su ballena de Greenpeace

Un sobre
no está
hecho de tinta
ni de lápiz.
ni de casas,
ni de números,
ni de calles o ciudades o paises.

Es un sobre
enviado
una vida
que comienza
en un archivo
en una carta de amor,
en un beso,
en un cheque reciclado
en un cobro por la historia,
en un beso por la ballena de Greenpeace,
o un vendedor por carta,
en un agradecimiento
una calumnia,
un deseo.

Un sobre es un
futuro poema
que envuelve
al mundo entre las cuatro
paredes
del pápel con que se mira,
doblado con sus dos brazos
y sus dos piernas,
esperando
que una canción
de manos sepa llevarlo
a su destinación.

My son thinks we are cows

Watching the Farmworkers
My son thinks we are cows
bent over in four legs
over fields.

The landscape moving
to the past in the car.

It is long ago he made
an identifiable tear in my eyes
gluing his lips to say "mommy cow".

Their back bones folded
like gymnasts
accrobating
forward
presenting their work
to strawberries and lettuce,
an audience full of perfume,
deodorants,
and other misused cosmetics.

"Mira las vacas mami
pisando las fresas"

Don't Misunderstand Her!
   Para las dos Y's de mi vida: Yvonne y Yolanda

Her tea speaks of
leaves that are books, not dregs
cards that fill hearts, not games
hands that are only stained
of polished truth
fingers that like paint brushes
point only at the colors
she can read,
the chalkboards she can translate,
the libraries she immerses in,
the minds she transgresses
the pain she magically turns
into fire.
Her fire is not singular
or present future past,
it is a photograph
she keeps in her desk
for when she needs to burn glass,
walk on blood
dress the saints in peace,
like Buddhists,
disrobe her soul
through laughter,
love.
Love to her is "turn the page" gentleness,
write this life before you start the next,
shave your legs only as a mantric exercise,
sneeze to capture a moment in time, a gaze, a peach
blossom before it
becomes a peach, like Chekhov's cherry blossoms.
Love only if it means circles like rosaries,
one mystery at a time
touch only if you mean to touch.

I was typing up this poem in response to Harold Shaw's comments about Watsonville, but I did not have the original article when my mother's neighbor María knocked at the door and gave me the Piñata Politics article from the Metro in which Mr. Shaw is introduced as Aptos candidate for the Pajaro Valley Unified School Dist Board of Trustees and is quoted as saying "Watsonville is doomed...There are lots of illegals, welfare fraud, heroin all over the place... and bars on almost every corner...There's a foreign race coming across the border...the Joses and Marias with their campesino mentality." With my campesina mentality I wrote this in response to his saying, "Watsonville is taken over by Catholics, Latinos and people intermarried to Mexicans," thinking about mixed marriages, my two sons, the sons of a mexicana and a gringo mexican lover.

They are mixed, they are charros in a car!

Love on love
language upon language
history with history
skin over skin

my sons, they are mixed
they are charros in a car
charros in carros,
fieldworker blood, teacher blood
cannery worker and engineer blood
musician and actress
jazz and rancheras
danzones, Frank,
huapangos Aretha,
Enrico Caruso and Jorge Vargas' mix
Marga Lopez and Christian Martell daiquiri

Cagualis of Buddha and
Thanksgiving turkey
stuffing
The Prophet, Jane Aire,
Amado Nervo, Langston Hughes blend
Robertson Davies, César Chavez, Philadelphia Square
Le Rouge et le Noir,
Guantanamera, Prague mixed,
hot chocolate, hoagies and peanut frijoles mixed

Do hearts grow when we water them
like toys
mending memories mixed
in a blender of love

Walking through the edge
of paper
waiting for the page to
turn
on multiracial ground
transcendent beams
waiting to be born
mixed only by thought.

Do hugs grow when we
color them
like broken bones
worshipping
the DNA of love

They are mole and salsa
mixed
mixed of appfelstruddel
and meat loaf mix
vegetarian lasagna and
low-fat I Can't Believe It's
Not Butter mix
the mime of Charlie
Chaplin
incompatible with
Cantinflas
too mixed to stop
a two continent belly laugh
loud as gold
grins of soul
IBM and Macintosh mixed
technology and education
mixed
love on love
language upon language
history with history
travel by travel
skin over skin mixed

Angela Davis and I

Privileged
I met Angela Davis when I was 12,
dancing rancheras with a Mexican at the Assumption
Church in Watsonville
Black power
church halled
my sister recognized Angela,
asked her for an autograph on envelope invitation
the flap of the envelope she once tried to sell at the Red
Barn flea market and no one bought
she had seen Angela on a wanted sign on TV
Angela and her black imaginary glove, a panther.
You told my sister to please not tell you were there,
"Groovy" said my sister in her teens,
you gave her the joy of importance.
Gloves-orange-yellow-white, and blue had only walked
the kitchens, canneries, hospitals and toilets of our minds.
And there they were Black Panthers, raising their black
hands in a black glove pointing to the sky
making God wear a black glove while pointing down at
us.
In my twenties college poverty years,
two times you saved me from not buying lunch:
a ten and a twenty fell out of your used books
I bought.
You wrote, saving me from losing every last bit of hope.
I made an altar to you in my thirties, community college
part-time, teaching poverty,
Migrant professor dignity
eight dollars for coffee fell out of the pages of your book,
I pregnant with no coffee in my purse,
you baked comfort for me.
Angela, now you are the last person I say goodbye to
while leaving my office when I shut down the light.
Your face is shiny black and white paper, dread locks,
hair, and hoops, And the twinkle in your teeth that spells
out justice.

Invaluable Tears or Professional Woman

It is not the redness of a rabbit eye contact lens
that makes you cry in your car
Or the soft way in which he touches
your legs on Sundays as you bike by

It is only a cell phone ringing,
your wail of a woman imitates,
A printer printing, that pants in your pain
A siren singing, after the death of a man
the rough movement of an untrained photocopier,
A Virgin in the act of love with a ditto.

An email is only as impatient
as a tear,
As fraudulent as an empty dollar bill

You in your office working through the rain
practicing your signature on books,
e-mailing volumes of your soul,
petting problems as they walk
knowing the rainbow is but a fax away,
An immigrant's impatient hour at the INS line,
A kiss is only transparent when it's copied
A heart is only palpitating as it writes

My Brown Toyota and Me Over 17
Highway 17 is a dangerous road between Santa Cruz and San Jose

You started it
by passing them up.
Those high heeled trucks or BMW jaguars,
or Mr. Commuter, I'm better because my car's apparently new.
You don't understand, It isn't that they think we want to go on 17,
we have to, we're supposed to be underprivileged right laners,
to them, we're old, we're brown, and we're women.
They don't see, we're 65 next to them,
on seventeen we're somehow invisible in speed but
neon-lit class, gender and raced.
Those businessmen bullies, those computer chip people
passing us up because we're going too slow at 70
their cars are babies, they don't see we've already gone to history and back.
They pass us up
because they think I'm poor and slow, you're brown and old.
They don't know we both have a new heart, yours a
privilege of the '92 Toyota body that crashed in Cresswell,
and the toothless mechanic that remembered,
mine, the fuel consumed from being a woman.
I would have liked to be slower because I'm brown, I know you say,
but I'm ahead of them, I've already had my heart patched up and it's doing well.
And me, I'm ahead of them
because I know my clutch can crack down at any moment.
We'll never catch up to them, Cost Co, hot dog eating middle classers,
or double decaf double fat free milk mongers,
we are two brown females up a windy four way road.

This is the way my father spelled Watsonville, making the town of his oppression holy

Guadsunvil

    I understand the power of tongues
      and torches
      and tremors
      and inundaciones.

I bought a strawberry   I understand economics
and stained my new   when I eat ollilaberry jam
silk Family Bargain Center   for
blouse   breakfast
             and the seeds attack me for

      dinner

I understand   I understand that these
strawberry fields
that lettuce fields   are forever but,
appear straight and become   don't make songs
crooked as they make   or are made into them.
monies

    I understand artichokes
     when they refuse
      to undress,
     so we could
       see
    only their heart.

  Since you are the Virgin's ugly brother,
      I understand
that she comes to visit you on oaks and through people
    because she can't stand you
      in person.

Curandera/Community Nurse
Para Olga Díaz

She's from a time
when sirens
are not cars.

Su corazón es
una jicama,
no sabe llorar,
es blanco,
denso y duro,
pero las cuerdas
de su canto
tiemblan
con el olor
a hospital.

Her heart
is a healer
by computer,
she spreads
lotion over
your wounds
and heals you,
prints you,
e-mails you,
communiqués
you to the Zapatistas,
pillows her politics,
her motherless pain.

She is a modern woman!

My Freedoms

My freedoms,
a car, some gas,
with which
to journey
back and forth
through my subconscious,

A dryer with which
to iron, an iron with
which to heat.

A computer with which
to comb my hair
inside the world's head.

A dishwasher with which
to wash a stone
to read my children's belly.

Nail polish
with which to paint
my thoughts on nails, frames and nylons.
Art, is all.

I Never Had A Picture Of My Parents/Surtout

And the bird in you swells in my throat
walking in crutches like a blind feeling
yawning under city lights:
"I never had a picture of my parents"
forgiving the dirt their love collapsed in,
knowing that my own child would forgive them,
not picturing their bond,
like a flower about to burp before an audience
forgives itself. Pasteles de postales,
pistolas de la historia
dulces, mentirosas, asesinas, deschavetados sin recuerdos
históricos.
Autrement je suis dans ma peau.
Autrement je chante du malheur des personnes savantes,
des personnes de toujours.
Autrement je sors de ma peau et je taquine la vie comme
un vieux qui bricole avec la pensée de son chien le plus
petit,
de son chien le plus lucide, surtout, et le plus chien,
qui a marre d'être personne
pour une fois.
Mais le monde révient a la langue toujours, comme un
sort de manoeuvre éparpillée, despavilada, desenredada,
desparramada,
en el cuerpo de una masa virginal que es la constatación
de una mentira sin límites.
Para nosotros los inmigrantes la vida es como una
gelatina que se guarda en el regrigerador en un recipiente
"tuperware"
que se saca y se sirve quince años después,
cuando los hijos están por estrenar cultura, con toda la
palabra,
que solo en nuestra cultura se estrena,
se externa,se es, permanentemente, se está practica y
logicamente al lado del vecino,que siempre puede hablar
su propia lengua, y la de los demás,que siempre nos
recuerda los malos ratos que pudieramos haber pasado si
no fueramos parte de él.
Para nosotros los inmigrantes no hay casa más nuestra
que la del vecino.

The 12th Commandment by a Mexican Woman

When people see me,
they always think of food.
I wish it were a picture or a paper
or even a metal I reminded them of.
But all of a sudden,
my face turns into a big flour tortilla, in their eyes.
My arms the other tortilla that hugs itself to feed them,
and my hands are asparagus and carrots, chiles and
cilantro ristras.
My butt, papas fritas con huevo
smelling up the space with food thoughts.
My stomach a molcajete,
grinding and blending up the salsa and guacamole for
them.
The only flower blooming about me is a margarita.
My feet the wine, my toes the grapes.
And as a working, milking, thinking, writing, loving,
computing, e-mailing woman
I say,
"Please don't eat me I am not a taco".

Their Country

In their own language
which is their country
my children
love themselves
in a toy
in three languages: poupée, train, nounours, trenecito,
teddy bear,

In a love: "Unforgettable, that's what you are..., caballito
blanco sácame de aquí, llévame a mi pueblo donde yo
nací, Tengo tengo tengo, tú no tienes nada, tengo tres
ovejas en una cabaña

mon petit cocotte, frère Jacques, frère Jacques chante une
chanson

in a flower- amapola bellísima amapola, no seas tan
ingrata llámame
amapola, amapola, cómo puedes tu vivir tan sola.

fleur, flor que no es nombre sino recuerdo - alouette
gentille alouette, rien, rien de rien, non je ne regrette
rien,

a memory of a memory
of a language
is their country.

California: Fresh as a Lettuce

I
She no longer loves.
The whites of her eyes fold
like a sheet,
sweat like a sheet,
and like a sheet,
cry at the hour of their
death.

II
Racism: sheetless bed,
not even a rag
or a cloth or a scent,
not even a picture con
safos
not what you do against
me or to me,
but what you didn't
manage to do,
didn't have time,
didn't make that phone
call for him,
didn't tell that friend about
her,
didn't have time
didn't will.

III
California,
not even a ghost
a doll, or a prayer,
not even an apple of
paradise,
or a yellow brick yard,
not even.

IV
Fresh as a lettuce
she sits on a slim-fast diet
getting her nails done,
filled in,
while they cut out our first
tongue
at the beauty parlour

V
Plastic surgery,
removing the growth of
culture
erasing the part of us
we remember without a
dictionary
She sits fresh as a lettuce
California, the woman,
man and child
getting her belly buton
pierced for her new gold
ring.

VI
Next week,
her urban skin tattooed
with a mute image of a
cleaning lady
just like a good dream
dark only on the outside
graffiti only on the inside,
fresh as a lettuce.

California Too

I burp before you
hamburgers, fries and hotdogs
I'm sorry!
I burp before you video games
inertia teens
zoomed
into MTV and rags.

I'm sorry!
I burp before you
politically correct racists
and diversity freaks, who play chess, fence, dance
flamenco
go out with rich browb women to prove a point.
I burp...
you hold the pickle
hold the lettuce on me
You like me to hold
my hard-working skills in high self-esteem
forty hours a week.
I go home,
I'm humble, as you wish, forty hours a week .
I make my lard tacos
only in my mind.
I buy olive oil only on weekends ,for company.
The rest of the time,
I hold the pickle, hold the lettuce on you.

I am an expert at holding vegetables before you.
I hear rumors
in rows a mile long.
Vegetables are their own best lawyers
in a salad bowl.

Sor Juana's Children

Your children
travel well.
They hide inside
soft faces of paper gowns,
from your hand into the land
of those who picture you an ageless leaf, a first
communion.

And, as I ovulate each month
I count and accrue my 264 eggs of a lifetime
that sing your poems
as they pass
into oblivion.

My eggs, the not so well written poems,
the tragic circles
that never learned to be,
aquatic,
the almost born inceptions
of a cobble stone
that chose to make an echo of a woman every time
we set foot on our monthly library carpet,
while your eggs look upon me from the shelf.

When I was a Wetback

I was a glass moon at the time, full of luck, love and longing
soft and transparent from the outside
a prickly fence inside
glass corners sticking out over the upper edges of my fence
ready to cut the tongue of the culprit with my humility
if ill will became him, but I never did.
I never bullied the bullies, lest the dogs bite my patent leather shoes.
I never combed my hair in public
I was cuddly with long braids Rapunzeling you to climb
to my brain, empty with questions
no doubts there about perfect bodies because every one was perfect.
My stretch marks from growing too fast and not eating
enough protein were beautiful roads
My stomach fat, a sponge to absorb the hurt of others,
my cushion of trust.
I passed used articles of clothing on to friends and family.
I enjoyed other's children on the bus
mended socks with holes with a light bulb, round. Threw away no thoughts.
Now that I am American
prickly only in my mind
no sharp corners here,
no perfect bodies in my house,
recycled glass of my fence keeps friends away a few feet,
The fence is higher than deeper.
I've learned to set limits, to cook only for pot lucks
to trust only on Ash Wednesday when truth begins to buy
cookies only from Girl Scouts, yesterday.
Before, only the Mexican men fried the fish in the patio
the women made rice, jello, and cake inside, I watched.

I knitted thoughts together
that would be useful for my new personality as an
American.
I prepared the yellow brick road with bricks of love and
food, yellow of bananas.
Sunshine of smiles fell within me like when you know
your mother knows you're beautiful and she won't tell
you, bananas of love.
But now, I fry the color yellow,
buy piñatas instead of mashé them,
sell at garage sales my memories for five cents,
charge my friends with their time for holding their babies,
throw out the rips of clothes, buy other people's
memories for ten cents.
Throw away my thoughts.

Enchiladas, Entomatadas, Chilaquiles

From the enchilada
ensebollada
into the world
vengo yo.
Me dieron de comer
the whole entomatada.
Me muero del empacho
de culturas
gue son los chilaquiles
sin queso. Learn to cook estadounidenses!

A todo esto:
No se puede vivir
sin la cebolla
aunque nos haga llorar.

Oda a Jose Antonio
Burciaga en Tres Partes

I
En lo blanco, verde, rojo
de su corazón
tiene una águila
que grita
"no dejen ahogarse a los demás."
En una águila pocha
que no tiene casa
en su espacio
porque
no tiene espacio
en su mundo,
es universal.
Es su brazo derecho
un tatuaje
Chalupa, Xochilmco
con nombre Cecilia
en su música y río
en su nave sentimental.
Sus dedos son hijos
que pintan y corren,
que escriben y lloran
a un hombre y a una mujer.

II
Los chistes nunca se
quedaron atrás.
Tienen venas y manos
y cabeza y techo,
pasan por las paredes de
la Gloria,
comen, respiran, cantan
igualdades rojas y negras y azules
con la confianza de lo que es
ser Dios en tierra ajena.

III
No pintas murales,
miramos alrededor
y somos el mural
que pintaste.
Sin darnos cuenta,
pero sabiendo
que vinimos de tu mano
y que a tu mano
la alimenta el papel
floreado de tu naturaleza
las carcajadas de los tiempos,
y la ternura de lo que es
ser producto tuyo.

Nos abrazamos
ya fuera del mural
en un beso eterno a tu
esencia.

About the Author

Gabriella Gutiérrez y Muhs is a Chicana multi-lingual poet, essayist, and author. She was first published in France at 18. She currently teaches at Seattle University and lives in the American Northwest, Aztlán, with her husband Eric and her two sons Eleuterio and Enrico. Gabriella is also a Chicana literary critic who specializes on theorizing Chicana subjectivity. Gabriella has held hundreds of poetry readings in schools, community events, prisons and universities, as well as for national organizations both in the United States and internationally. Her poetry has been taught in France and Spain, and she has read at prestigious arts festivals throughout the United States. Gabriella Gutiérrez y Muhs received the Calabash Award for Excellence in the Ethnic Arts in California in 2000. She once was la "Doctora Corazón" for a community radio program. It is her biggest claim to fame -- a heart.

New Women's Voices Series Collection by Finishing Line Press

NEW WOMEN'S VOICES SERIES CHAPBOOKS ISSN 1098-8173

Leah Maines' best selling chapbook *LOOKING TO THE EAST WITH WESTERN EYES*, NWV No. 1, paper ISBN 0-9664324-0-1 (Now in its third printing, 1998, 2000, 2002): $12.00 plus $2.00 S&H

Joyce Sidman's *LIKE THE AIR*, (1999) WINNER OF THE NEW WOMEN'S VOICES PRIZE IN POETRY, No. 2, paper ISBN 0-9664324-2-8: $9.00 PLUS $2.00 S&H

Gayle Pierce's *MAMA THOUGHTS* (2002) NWV No. 3. This title is now OUT OF PRINT.

Kathy Cantley Ackerman's *THE TIME IT TAKES*, "*The Time it Takes* celebrates the quiet intervals of our lives--the time between the monumental events, where truth lies."--Leah Maines (2002 LIMITED EDITION), NWV No.4, paper ISBN 0-9664324-8-7, $12.00 plus $2.00 S&H

Carol Barrett's *DRAWING LESSONS*, "Dr. Barrett's work is fluid and sublte yet also artistically pictorial and deeply visceral. . ."-- Jose Cedillos (2002 LIMITED EDITION) NWV No. 5, paper ISBN 0-9664324-9-5, $12.00 plus $2.00 S&H

Sandra Graff's *GIRL IN GARDEN*, "Girl in Garden shows us the beauty of the everyday--a birdbath, a child's socks, a colander--*what we might miss while a seemingly inconsequential brightness filters through.*" -- Melissa Montimurro (2002 Limited Edition) NWV No. 6, paper ISBN 0-9718922-0-2, $12.00 plus $2.00 S&H

Cheryl Snell's *FLOWER HALF BLOWN*, "*Flower Half Blown* blossoms into a poetic garden of discovery."--Leah Maines (2002 Limited Editon) NWV No. 7, paper ISBN 0-9718922-1-0, $12.00 plus $2.00 S&H

Christa Polkinhorn-Umiker's *PATH OF FIRE*, "*Path of Fire* is full of unsentimental but emotionally charged poems about loneliness and family and searching the earth for a home."--Gwynne Garfinkle (2002 Limited Edition) NWV No.8, paper ISBN 0-9718922-2-9, $12.00 plus $2.00 S&H

Gwen Hart's *LOSING OHIO*, " Gwen Hart's formidable skills unfold in Losing Ohio in both formal and free verse -- she has an unerring ear and an eye for the quirky details that make up everyday life."--

Allison Joseph, Poetry Editor, *Crab Orchard Review* (2002 Limited Edition) NWV No. 9, paper ISBN 0-9718922-5-3, $12.00 plus $2.00 S&H.

Joyce B. Adams' *SECRET SWING*, "Adams is a one-of-a-kind lyricist whose strong, unpretentious voice seems to have been with us for a long time."'--Daniel G. Ford (2002 Limited Edition) NWV No. 10, paper, ISBN 0-9718922-8-8, $12.00 plus $2.00 S&H.

Helen Mallon's *BONE CHINA*, "Both the poet and her people are sometimes *cloaked in layers. The detail in these poems is rich, the language fresh and,* often, anguished."--Henry Braun NWV No. 11, paper, $12.00 plus $2.00 S&H.

Phyllis Berman's *MOONGATE*, "With the delicacy and wisdom of those Chinese poets she so admires, Phyllis Berman has given us an astonishing and gorgeous cycle of poems."--David St. John NWV No. 12, paper, $12.00 plus $2.00 S&H.

Sherry Chandler's *DANCE THE BLACK-EYED GIRL*, "Reading these poems is like visiting with a cherished family member, the one who knows, just back from the reunion and the general store with a report or two on things as they are."--James Baker Hall, Kentucky Poet Laureate. **NWV No. 13, $12.00, paper, ISBN 0-9726136-7-6. ORDER BEFORE FEB. 17 AND GET FREE SHIPPING.**

How to Order

Send Check or Money Order to:
Finishing Line Press
Post Office Box 1626
Georgetown, Ky. 40324